by Iain Gray

PUBLISHING

WRITING *to* REMEMBER

Lang**Syne**

PUBLISHING

WRITING *to* REMEMBER

Vineyard Business Centre,
Pathhead, Midlothian EH37 5XP
Tel: 01875 321 203 Fax: 01875 321 233
E-mail: info@lang-syne.co.uk
www.langsyneshop.co.uk

Design by Dorothy Meikle
Printed by Ricoh Print Scotland
© Lang Syne Publishers Ltd 2010

ISBN 978-1-85217-366-1

Allan

MOTTO:
God will direct it
(and)
I hope.

CREST:
An arm with the hand
grasping a scimitar
(and)
the hunting and tracking
hound known as a talbot.

NAME variations include:
Alan
Allen
Allison
Callan
MacAllan

*Echoes of a far distant past
can still be found in most names*

Chapter one:

Origins of
Scottish surnames

by George Forbes

It all began with the Normans.

For it was they who introduced surnames into common usage more than a thousand years ago, initially based on the title of their estates, local villages and chateaux in France to distinguish and identify these landholdings, usually acquired at the point of a bloodstained sword.

Such grand descriptions also helped enhance the prestige of these arrogant warlords and generally glorify their lofty positions high above the humble serfs slaving away below in the pecking order who only had single names, often with Biblical connotations as in Pierre and Jacques.

The only descriptive distinctions among this peasantry concerned their occupations, like Pierre the swineherd or Jacques the ferryman.

The Normans themselves were originally Vikings (or Northmen) who raided, colonised and eventually settled down around the French coastline.

They had sailed up the Seine in their longboats in 900 AD under their ferocious leader Rollo and ruled the roost in north east France before sailing over to conquer England, bringing their relatively new tradition of having surnames with them.

It took another hundred years for the Normans to percolate northwards and surnames did not begin to appear in Scotland until the thirteenth century.

These adventurous knights brought an aura of chivalry with them and it was said no damsel of any distinction would marry a man unless he had at least two names.

The family names included that of Scotland's great hero Robert De Brus and his compatriots were warriors from families like the De Morevils, De Umphravils, De Berkelais, De Quincis, De Viponts and De Vaux.

As the knights settled the boundaries of their vast estates, they took territorial names, as in Hamilton, Moray, Crawford, Cunningham, Dunbar, Ross, Wemyss, Dundas, Galloway, Renfrew, Greenhill, Hazelwood, Sandylands and Church-hill.

Other names, though not with any obvious geographical or topographical features, nevertheless derived from ancient parishes like Douglas, Forbes, Dalyell and Guthrie.

Other surnames were coined in connection with occupations, castles or legendary deeds. Stuart originated in the word steward, a prestigious post which was an integral part of any large medieval household. The same applied to Cooks, Chamberlains, Constables and Porters.

Borders towns and forts – needed in areas like the Debateable Lands which were constantly fought over by feuding local families – had their own distinctive names; and it was often from them that the resident groups took their communal titles, as in the Grahams of Annandale, the Elliots and Armstrongs of the East Marches, the Scotts and Kerrs of Teviotdale and Eskdale.

Even physical attributes crept into surnames, as in Small, Little and More (the latter being 'beg' in Gaelic), Long or Lang, Stark, Stout, Strong or Strang and even Jolly.

Mieklejohns would have had the strength of several men, while Littlejohn was named after the legendary sidekick of Robin Hood.

Colours got into the act with Black, White, Grey, Brown and Green (Red developed into Reid,

Ruddy or Ruddiman). Blue was rare and nobody ever wanted to be associated with yellow.

Pompous worthies took the name Wiseman, Goodman and Goodall.

Words intimating the sons of leading figures were soon affiliated into the language as in Johnson, Adamson, Richardson and Thomson, while the Norman equivalent of Fitz (from the French-Latin 'filius' meaning 'son') cropped up in Fitzmaurice and Fitzgerald.

The prefix 'Mac' was 'son of' in Gaelic and clans often originated with occupations – as in MacNab being sons of the Abbot, MacPherson and MacVicar being sons of the minister and MacIntosh being sons of the chief.

The church's influence could be found in the names Kirk, Clerk, Clarke, Bishop, Friar and Monk. Proctor came from a church official, Singer and Sangster from choristers, Gilchrist and Gillies from Christ's servant, Mitchell, Gilmory and Gilmour from servants of St Michael and Mary, Malcolm from a servant of Columba and Gillespie from a bishop's servant.

The rudimentary medical profession was represented by Barber (a trade which also once included dentistry and surgery) as well as Leech or Leitch.

Businessmen produced Merchants, Mercers, Monypennies, Chapmans, Sellers and Scales, while down at the old village watermill the names that cropped up included Miller, Walker and Fuller.

Other self explanatory trades included Coopers, Brands, Barkers, Tanners, Skinners, Brewsters and Brewers, Tailors, Saddlers, Wrights, Cartwrights, Smiths, Harpers, Joiners, Sawyers, Masons and Plumbers.

Even the scenery was utilised as in Craig, Moor, Hill, Glen, Wood and Forrest.

Rank, whether high or low, took its place with Laird, Barron, Knight, Tennant, Farmer, Husband, Granger, Grieve, Shepherd, Shearer and Fletcher.

The hunt and the chase supplied Hunter, Falconer, Fowler, Fox, Forrester, Archer and Spearman.

The renowned medieval historian Froissart, who eulogised about the romantic deeds of chivalry (and who condemned Scotland as being a poverty stricken wasteland), once sniffily dismissed the peasantry of his native France as the jacquerie (or the jacques-without-names) but it was these same humble folk who ended up overthrowing the arrogant aristocracy.

In the olden days, only the blueblooded knights of antiquity were entitled to full, proper names, both Christian and surnames, but with the passing of time and a more egalitarian, less feudal atmosphere, more respectful and worthy titles spread throughout the populace as a whole.

Echoes of a far distant past can still be found in most names and they can be borne with pride in commemoration of past generations who fought and toiled in some capacity or other to make our nation what it now is, for good or ill.

Chapter two:

Kinsfolk and Covenanters

A name found from earliest times from the Scottish Borders to the Highlands and Islands, 'Allan' is the most common form found in Scotland, with the variant 'Allen' more popular south of the Border and in North America.

Other variants include Alan and Callan, while there is also the Scottish-Gaelic form of 'MacAllan.'

There are at least two quite different meanings of the name, one of them uniquely Scottish, in that it is thought to derive from the Old Gaelic 'ailin', indicating a rock, while another possible derivation is from a popular Germanic name indicating 'handsome.'

The name was also popular with those Normans who settled in England in the wake of the Norman Conquest of 1066, and a family of the name became established in Lincolnshire.

In common with many other Anglo-Norman families, branches of the Allans took up landholdings in Scotland in the twelfth century at the invitation of the Scottish monarch David I, but it should be stressed that bearers of the name, originally in the form of 'MacAllan', were already firmly established there.

Evidence that 'Allans' were present in Scotland before the influx of Anglo-Norman bearers of the name comes through the fact that bearers of the Allan/MacAllan name are recognised as a sept, or sub-branch, of at least two ancient and distinguished Scottish clans.

These are MacDonald of Clanranald and Clan MacFarlane, although some sources assert that the Allans are also a sept of Clan Grant and Clan MacKay.

Whatever the veracity of the assertion, what is known for certain is that it was with the MacDonalds and the MacFarlanes that the Allans appear to have enjoyed the closest kinship.

As a sept of these clans, bearers of the Allan name are entitled to share not only their proud heritage and traditions, but also entitled to adopt their respective mottoes and crests and wear their tartan.

But not all Allans of today are necessarily a sept of the same clan.

To determine which clan their ancestors

originally 'belonged', it would be necessary to attempt to trace their original territory.

The Northern Isles and northwest Argyll is the original territory of the MacDonalds of Clanranald, whose motto is 'My hope is constant in thee', and crest a hand wielding a sword, emerging from a triple-towered castle.

The territory of the MacFarlanes – motto of 'This I'll defend' and crest of a naked savage wielding a sword – was for centuries the Loch Lomond area.

As a sept of these clans, the Allans shared in both their glorious fortunes and tragic misfortunes – with MacFarlanes and many of their kinsfolk such as the Allans among the 5,000 Scots killed at the disastrous battle of Flodden in September of 1513.

Those Allans who were kinsfolk of the MacDonalds of Clanranald, one of the first clans to rally to the doomed cause of Bonnie Prince Charlie, were also among the many Jacobite dead at the equally disastrous battle of Culloden in April of 1746.

Earlier, in the seventeenth century, a number of Allans also died fighting for their religious beliefs.

A National Covenant, pledging defence of the Presbyterian religion, had been signed in the Greyfriars Kirkyard, in Edinburgh, in February of 1638.

Copies were circulated throughout Scotland, and the hundreds of ordinary men and women who subscribed to it became known as Covenanters.

Following the restoration to the throne of Charles II in 1660, the death knell for the Covenanting movement was sounded when a Recissory Act was passed, declaring the Covenant illegal.

Episcopal rule was foisted on the Scottish Church, and all ministers who refused to adhere to this new order were deprived of their parishes.

Along with their congregations, many ministers literally took to the hills, preaching at open-air meetings known as conventicles.

Lookouts were posted to keep a wary eye out for the approach of Government troops, and justice was executed on the spot for those unfortunate enough to fall into Government hands.

Many of the memorials scattered across the hills and valleys of Lowland Scotland mark the very spots where victims were summarily shot and unceremoniously buried.

Constantly persecuted by the forces of authority, the Covenanters rose in futile rebellion in November of 1666 and, as a sign of the harsh treatment that was to be subsequently meted out to them, many of the prisoners taken were tortured and hanged.

Victory followed at the battle of Drumclog in June of 1679, only to be followed a few short weeks later by resounding defeat at the battle of Bothwell Brig, near Hamilton, by a force commanded by the Duke of Monmouth.

Nearly 800 Covenanters were killed and 1,400 taken prisoner.

Kept for several weeks in open cages in Greyfriars Kirkyard, prisoners who agreed to sign a bond for future 'good behaviour' were released, but by November of 1679 more than 250 steadfastly recalcitrant prisoners still remained.

These included a John Allan and six other Covenanters from the parish of Torphichen, in West Lothian.

The authorities decided to sell them as slaves on the steaming plantations of Barbados, and arrangements were accordingly made to transport them there aboard the *Crown of London*.

But the vessel foundered on December 10th off the headland of Scarva Taing, near the Mull Head of Deerness, in Orkney, during a violent storm, and John Allan was among the estimated 209 prisoners who drowned while still locked below decks.

A memorial to the martyrdom of Allan and his fellow Covenanters was erected by public subscription on the bleakness of Scarva Taing in 1888.

Dynasties of wealthy and influential bearers of the Allan name became established in the Lowlands and Borders of Scotland, adopting their own Coats of Arms as symbols of their prestige.

An Allan family based in the Glasgow area, for example, adopted the motto 'I hope', and the crest of the head of a hunting and tracking dog known as a talbot.

One particularly notable family of the name is that of the Allans of Hillside and Glen, whose motto is 'God will direct it', and whose crest is an arm with the hand grasping a scimitar.

The founder of this dynasty was Alexander Allan, born in 1746 near Prestonpans, on the outskirts of Edinburgh, and who died in 1825.

He is recorded as having been admitted as a burgess of Edinburgh in 1772, around the same time he founded the bank of Alexander Allan and Co., with offices in the capital's Princes Street and High Street.

The wealth he accrued as a banker and merchant allowed him to buy the 3,500-acre estate of

Glen, near Innerleithen, in the County of Peebles, in 1796, while his six-acre Hillside estate, located south of Edinburgh's Calton Hill, was later developed between 1821 and 1823 as part of the city's second New Town.

One indication of his wealth and social prestige is that he and his wife and daughter were all painted by the great Scottish portrait artist Sir Henry Raeburn.

Also of the same family of bankers and merchants was the pioneering mineralogist Thomas Allan, born in Edinburgh in 1777.

In addition to pursuing a career in the family business, he also travelled widely to collect and study minerals, and one he discovered in Greenland was subsequently named *Allanite* in his honour.

A Fellow of the Royal Societies of both Edinburgh and London, he died in 1833, while his vast collection of minerals was later donated to the British Museum of Natural History, and in whose care it remains to this day.

Chapter three:

Fame and fortune

It was on the battlefield that another member of the Allans of Hillside and Glen family gained distinction.

This was Major General William Allan, who was born in Edinburgh's Hillside Crescent in 1832.

Serving with the 41st Foot throughout the Crimean War of 1853 to 1856, he was present at a number of notable engagements, including the battle of Alma and the battle of Inkerman.

Also present at the siege and fall of Sebastopol, he was later awarded the French Légion d'Honneur, and went on to serve from 1890 to 1894 as Commander of British Troops in Cyprus.

A member of a family of Allans from Ayrshire, Colonel Alexander Allan, born at Rosebank, Ayr, in 1888, and a friend of the poet of the First World War, Rupert Brooke, served throughout that conflict with the Queen's Own Cameron Highlanders.

Later transferring to the Royal Corps of Signals, he served as Chief Signals Officer, Western

Command, from 1929 to 1933; a recipient of the Military Cross (MC), he died in 1967.

Bearers of the Allan name have gained fame and fortune far from Scottish shores in the world of commerce.

One of the wealthiest men in the world and the richest man in Canada at the time of his death in 1882, Sir Hugh Allan was the entrepreneur who was born in 1810 in Saltcoats, Ayrshire.

His father, Alexander Allan, born in 1780 and a first cousin of Scotland's national bard Robert Burns, began his working life as a carpenter on an estate at Fairlie, in Ayrshire. He later became the master of a small ship, or brig, laying the foundation of the Allan Shipping Line, running goods from the Scottish west coast port of Greenock to Montreal, and returning with Canadian goods.

Hugh Allan began working for his father in 1823, but three years later went to work in Montreal for the grain merchant William Kerr, one of his father's business partners.

By 1835, he had become a partner in the Montreal importing firm of Millar, Edmonstone and Co; eventually taking over its shipping operation with the financial backing of his family back in Scotland.

Later joined by his brother Andrew, he soon added to the Allan Shipping Line with his Montreal Ocean Steamship Company, which had the lucrative contract to take mail to and from Montreal to London and to and from Montreal to the American port of Portland, in Maine.

Meanwhile another brother, James, had taken over from his father, running the Allan Shipping Line's Greenock base, while another brother, Bryce, was in charge of the company's Liverpool base.

The ever-enterprising Hugh Allan also branched out into railways, and by the 1870s had created a syndicate to build Canada's national railway.

Also a director of the Bank of Montreal, he was knighted by Queen Victoria in 1871, eleven years before his death in his native Scotland while visiting relatives in Edinburgh.

On his death, the Allan business empire was taken over by his brother, Andrew, before control passed to Sir Hugh's second son, Hugh Montagu Allan.

Born in Montreal in 1860 and better known as H. Montagu Allan, in addition to his role with the Allan Shipping Line, he also became president of a number of other enterprises that included the

Canadian Rubber Company, the Carlton Hotel Company and the Canadian Paper Company.

Knighted in 1906, he also served in France during the First World War as a Lieutenant Colonel of the Canadian Expeditionary Force.

Allan, who died in 1951, was also a keen sportsman and avid fan of the Canadian national sport of ice hockey and, in 1906, donated what is known as the Allan Cup – awarded annually to this day to Canada's senior amateur ice hockey champions.

His cousin, Lady Isobel Meredith, meanwhile in 1920 donated the Lady Meredith Cup, the first ice hockey trophy to be competed for by female players.

Another prominent Canadian entrepreneur of Scottish roots was William Allan, who was born in 1770 near Huntly, in Aberdeenshire.

Immigrating to Canada at the age of 17, by 1795 he was settled in York (now Toronto) in business partnership with fellow Scot Alexander Wood.

By the time of his death in 1853, he had risen to become a leading Canadian banker, businessman and politician.

In the world of engineering, Alexander Allan, who was born in 1809 in Montrose, Angus, was the Scottish mechanical engineer who invented both the balanced slide valve and the straight-link valve gear for railway engines.

Locomotive superintendent of the Scottish General Railway from 1853 to 1865, he died in 1891.

Bearers of the Allan name have also excelled in the creative world of art.

Known as 'the Scottish Hogarth' in reference to the comic and satirical works of the English painter William Hogarth, David Allan was the Scottish painter who was born in 1744 in Alloa, Clackmannanshire, and died in 1796.

It was after studying painting for seven years at the Foulis Academy of Painting in Glasgow that he received the valuable patronage of Lord Cathcart and Lord Erskine of Mar, allowing him to travel to Rome in 1764 and spend a number of years studying and copying Old Masters.

The main fruit of this was his painting *The Origin of Portraiture*, now one of the prized exhibits in the National Gallery of Scotland, in Edinburgh.

Appointed director and master of the Academy of Arts in Edinburgh in 1786, he executed a number of portrait commissions, but remains best known for humorous and mildly satirical historical paintings that include *Illustrations of the Gentle*

Shepherd, *Repentance Stool*, *Highland Dance*, and his 1780 *The Highland Wedding*.

Yet another distinguished painter of the Allan name was William Allan, who was born in Edinburgh in 1782.

Travelling throughout the vast expanse of Russia from 1805 to 1814 and capturing on canvas the lives of ordinary Russians, he later returned to his native Scotland and turned his talents to depicting characters and scenes from its turbulent history.

A friend of the novelist Sir Walter Scott, he illustrated scenes from some of his writings, one example of which is his 1827 *The Black Dwarf*.

Several of his works are in the care of the National Gallery of Scotland, while his 1824 Russian work *Bashkirs* is in the care of the Hermitage Museum in St Petersburg.

A president of the Royal Scottish Academy, he died in 1850.

Chapter four:

On the world stage

Bearers of the Allan name and its variations such as Allen have gained distinction through a wide range of activities, not least through the medium of film.

Born in 1935 in Brooklyn, New York, Allen Stewart Konisberg is the multi-talented American actor, comedian, film director, screenwriter, playwright and jazz clarinettist better known as **Woody Allen**.

From writing short stories and cartoon captions for magazines such as *The New Yorker*, Allen went on to star in and produce memorable films that include the 1977 *Annie Hall*, the 1979 *Manhattan*, the 1994 *Bullets over Broadway* and, from 2005, *Match Point*.

The star of nearly fifty films over a 25-year period, **Elizabeth Allan** was the English actress born in 1908 in Skegness, Lincolnshire.

Her many film roles include the 1935 *David Copperfield* and the 1953 adaptation of novelist Graham Greene's *The Heart of the Matter*, while she was also a regular panellist on British television shows such as *What's My Line?*

The actress, who was named Great Britain's Top Female TV Personality of 1952, died in 1990.

Stunt co-ordinator for the 2009 film *Scott Pilgrim vs. the World*, **Bradley Allan** is the Australian actor, stunt performer, martial artist and action choreographer who was born in 1973 in Melbourne, while **Elkan Allan** was a leading British television producer.

Born in 1922, Allan, who died in 2006, is best known as the creator of the 1960s British television popular music show *Ready Steady Go!*

Also on television, **Dave Allen** was the stage name of the Irish comedian and satirist David Tynan O'Mahoney, who was born in Dublin in 1936 and died in 2005.

Born in Toronto in 1873, Beulah Maude Durrant was the actress, dancer and choreographer better known as **Maude Allan**.

She adopted the name in a bid to distance herself in the eyes of the public from her notorious brother Theodore Durrant, who was hanged in San Francisco in 1898 for the sensational murder of two women.

Allan herself also gained a degree of notoriety during her lifetime.

In 1900 she published an illustrated sex manual for women while, billed as the Salomé Dancer, six years later she performed her erotic *Dance of the Seven Veils*, based on the playwright Oscar Wilde's *Salomé*; she died in 1956.

Also on the stage, **Jed Allan** is the American actor who was one of the stars of the *Lassie* television series from 1968 to 1970.

Born in 1937 in New York, he is also known for his role from 1971 to 1985 as Don Craig in the television series *Days of Our Lives*, while he also appeared from 1986 to 1993 in the series *Santa Barbara*.

Across the Atlantic, **Andrea Allan** is the Scottish actress who was born in Glasgow in 1946.

With roles in many British comedy films of the 1960s and 1970s such as *Carry on Spying* and, with Dudley Moore, *The Wrong Box*, she also appeared in television series that include *Gideon's Way*, *Space 1999* and *Jason King*.

Although he has had roles in American television dramas such as *CSI: Miami* and *Desperate Housewives*, **Hunter Allan**, born in 1995 in Fort Myers, Florida, is the young American actor best known for his role on the CBS television soap *The Young and the Restless*.

On radio, **Andrew Allan**, who was born in Scotland in 1907 and later immigrated to Canada, served as the national head of the Canadian Broadcasting Corporation (CBC) Drama from 1943 to 1955.

He died in 1974, and the old wooden armchair that served as his office chair at CBC's Toronto headquarters is handed down from one head of drama to the next.

Back to acting, **Keith Allen** is the actor, comedian, musician and television presenter who was born in Swansea, Wales, in 1953.

In the early 1980s he had roles in a number of *The Comic Strip Presents* films, made by Channel 4 Television, while other television credits include *Martin Chuzzlewit*, adapted for the BBC in 1996, and, from 2006 to 2009, the role of the Sheriff of Nottingham in *Robin Hood*.

He is the father of the top recording artist **Lily Allen**, who was born in London in 1985.

Also the host of a television talk show, *Lily Allen and Friends*, her 2006 debut album *Alright, Still*, gained her nominations at the Grammy, MTV Music Video and BRIT awards.

Also in the world of contemporary music, **James Allan**, born in 1979 in Dalmarnock, Glasgow, is the lead singer of the Scottish rock band Glasvegas, whose hits include *Daddy's Gone* and *Flowers and Football Tops*.

A professional footballer until he formed the band in 2003, he played for teams that include Falkirk, Stirling and Queen's Park; keeping it in the family, his cousin Rab Allan is a guitarist with the band, while his sister Denise manages it.

On the field of battle, **William Allen** was an English recipient of the Victoria Cross, the highest award for bravery for British and Commonwealth forces. He was serving with the 2nd Battalion, 24th Regiment of Foot, during the Zulu Wars, when the regiment came under Zulu attack at Rorke's Drift, in Natal, in January of 1879.

Allen, who had been reduced from the rank of sergeant to corporal for previously being drunk on duty, won his award for helping to evacuate wounded comrades from the base hospital.

Born in 1844, he died in 1890.

In a later conflict, yet another **William Allen** was also a recipient of the Victoria Cross.

Born in Sheffield in 1892, he was a captain in the Royal Army Medical Corps during the First World War when, in September of 1916 near Mesnil, in

France, he ignored very heavy shellfire and his own wounds to tend wounded comrades.

He died in 1933, and his Victoria Cross is displayed in the British Army Medical Museum in Aldershot.

From the field of battle to the highly competitive world of sport, **Stephen Allan** is the Australian professional golfer of Scottish parentage who was born in 1973 in Melbourne.

A member of the European Tour from 1997 to 2000, he also won the German Open in 1998 and the 2000 Australian Open.

In the rough and tumble of rugby, **James Allan** was the New Zealand rugby union forward nicknamed the "Taieri Giant".

Born in Taieri in 1860, Allan, who died in 1934, played eight games during his career for the New Zealand national team, the All Blacks.

Also on the rugby pitch, **Trevor Allan**, born in 1926 in Bathurst, New South Wales, was the Australian player who captained the national rugby union team on 40 occasions between 1946 and 1949 before switching to rugby league.

Following his retirement from the game, he pursued a successful career as a rugby commentator and was awarded the Order of Australia for his services to the game.

He died in 2007, following which Australia's rugby competition known as the Trevor Allan Cup was created in his honour.

On the fields of European football, **James Allan** was the Scottish schoolteacher and footballer who was born in Ayr in 1857 and who died in 1911.

Moving to Sunderland as a teacher, he was appointed headmaster of Hendon Board School and, in October of 1879, founded Sunderland and District teachers' Association Football Club, for which he played and which later became better known as the English club Sunderland A.F.C.

In the creative world of literature, **Peter John Allan**, born in 1825 in York, England, and whose family later immigrated to Canada, was the young poet whose work was published after his death in 1848 as *The poetical remains of Peter John Allan*, while **William Allan** is the distinguished Scottish classicist who specialises in Greek epic and tragedy.

Born in 1970, he is a former assistant professor of classics at Harvard University and, at the time of writing, tutor in Greek and Latin languages and literature at University College, Oxford.

The author of more than 130 books for children, **Mabel Allan**, born in 1915, was the English writer who also wrote under the pen names of Jean Estoril, Priscilla Hagon and Anne Pilgrim.

Author of books that include the 1948 *The Glen Castle Mystery*, she died in 1998.

In a different writing genre, **Angus Allan**, born in 1936 in Wimbledon, London, and who died in 2007, was the British comic strip writer best known for penning many of the *Garth* adventures for the Daily Mirror newspaper.

In the world of politics, **John Allan**, born in 1866 near Lancefield, Victoria, was the Australian politician of Scottish roots who served as 29th Premier of Victoria from 1924 to 1927 – Australia's first Country Party Premier; he died in 1936.

Born in 1914, **Robert Allan** was the British Conservative Party politician who served as MP for Paddington between 1951 and 1966 and who died in 1979.

Created a life peer in 1973 as Baron Allan of Kilmahew of Cardross in the County of Dunbartonshire, at the time of writing his son, **Alexander Allan**, is chairman of the Joint Intelligence Committee and head of Intelligence Assessment in the United Kingdom.

Born in 1921, **Sir Colin Allan** was the New Zealand politician who served as Governor of the Seychelles from 1973 to 1975 and Governor of the Solomon Islands from 1976 to 1978; he died in 1998.

The Allan name is also to be found on the landscape in the form of the name of a small town in Canada's west central Saskatchewan, as a commune in the Drôme department in south-eastern France, and through **Bridge of Allan** – a town to the north of Stirling in the ancient Allan homeland of Scotland.